واحة السلام   נווה שלום

by Laurie Dolphin · Photographs by Ben Dolphin

SCHOLASTIC INC. *NEW YORK*

SCHOLASTIC HARDCOVER

To the memory of my friend Candy Jernigan
—L.D.

To my sons, Brian and Miles,
may you have the vision and courage
to make the effort to understand yourselves and others.
Only in so doing will our world's future be assured
—B.D.

This is Shlomo Frankin. Shlomo is a Hebrew name that means "peace." Shlomo is named after King Solomon, who kept the Jews out of war for forty years.

At home and in school, Shlomo's friends and family have nicknamed him Shlomki.

Shlomki is ten and a half years old. He is Jewish and lives in Israel.

This is Muhammad Jabar. The name Muhammad means "the praised one." It is also the name of the prophet who started the Islamic religion.

Muhammad is ten and a half years old. He is an Arab Moslem and also lives in Israel.

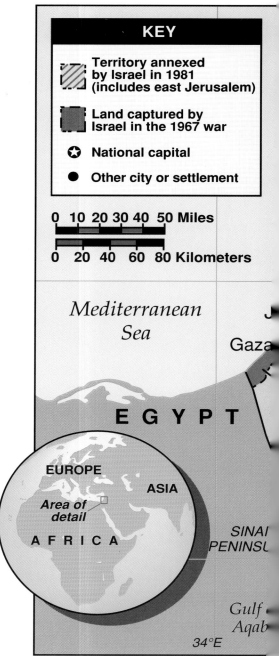

KEY

Territory annexed by Israel in 1981 (includes east Jerusalem)

Land captured by Israel in the 1967 war

★ National capital

● Other city or settlement

0 10 20 30 40 50 Miles

0 20 40 60 80 Kilometers

Mediterranean Sea

Gaza

EGYPT

EUROPE

ASIA

Area of detail

AFRICA

SINAI PENINSU

Gulf Aqab

34°E

Israel is a tiny country that connects the continent of Asia to Africa. It is about the same size as New Jersey.

Since the birth of the State of Israel in 1948, Arabs and Jews have fought over this land. They both believe this country is their homeland. They are having a hard time sharing it.

Israel is always prepared for war. Soldiers with guns are still seen throughout the country. Arabs and Jews live in fear of each other.

Like most Arabs and Jews, Shlomki and Muhammad live in their own villages and go to their own separate schools. Their religions and customs are different. They even speak in different languages, and yet they live together in Israel.

Soon they will meet each other, but first let us see where and how they live.

Muhammad lives in Abu Ghosh. Abu Ghosh is an old Arab village right outside of Jerusalem. It is said that all the people from Abu Ghosh are related because they are descendants of the same family. Over five thousand Arabs live there now.

Muhammad has a large family. He has five older brothers and one older sister. His extended family includes fourteen aunts and nine uncles.

His older sister, Linda, is married with one baby. She and her husband want to have a small family. They want only two children. Muhammad is proud to be a young uncle, and his parents are proud grandparents.

In the daytime, Muhammad's mom, Yusra, runs a small daycare center in her home.

Muhammad's dad, Selim, is a contractor. He has built many houses outside of Jerusalem. He has even built his own home.

Inside their house, there is a wall with pieces of stones from all of the houses Selim has built.

Outside the house, Muhammad has many
pets. He has a horse called Micky, a dog
called Lacks, and four ducks.

In the center of Abu Ghosh is a mosque where Arab Moslems pray. Every day from the mosque, five times a day, prayers can be heard from a loudspeaker. The prayers are at dawn, noon, afternoon, sunset, and early evening.

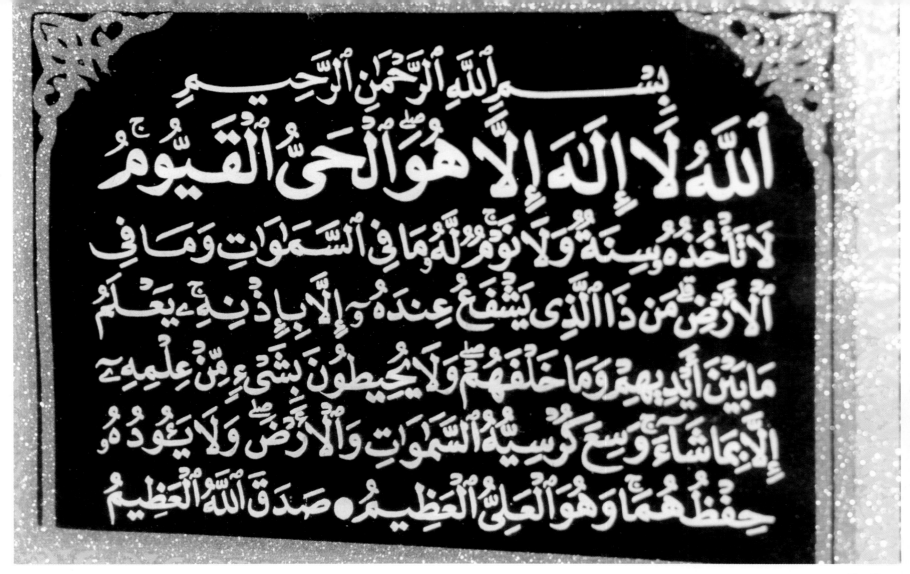

The Koran

Muhammad's family is not religious, and yet they do celebrate certain holidays. For the month of Ramadan, from sunrise to sunset, they do not eat. This is called fasting. After the sun sets, a large meal is served each night during this month. Also during this month the Koran is read from start to finish, and Moslems thank God for his goodness.

13

When the month of Ramadan is over, there is a big celebration and feast at Muhammad's house. All his relatives throughout Abu Ghosh come to his home.

Yusra and her female relatives cook in the kitchen. Lamb and rice with tomato sauce is a favorite dish. The meat is served with laban, which is a thin, liquid yogurt. Moslems eat milk with meat. The Jews do not eat the two together. Moslems, like the Jews, do not eat pork.

Muhammad's best friend is also his cousin. They go to the same Arab school together in Abu Ghosh.

Next year, Muhammad's mom and dad have decided to send him to a different school. This school is very special. It is a school where Jews and Arabs learn together peacefully.

For peace in Israel, Muhammad's parents want him to meet Jewish children, learn Hebrew, and make Jewish friends. Only in this school is that a possibility.

Muhammad is scared of going. He knows that he will miss his Arab friends at his old school. He will especially miss his best friend. Muhammad has never had any Jewish friends and wonders whether they will like him.

Let us now visit Shlomki at his home.

Shlomki lives in a Jewish village called Nataf. About sixty families live here. Nataf is a village where religious and nonreligious Jews live together.

This is Shlomki's brother, Elia, who is six and a half. His sister, Reuma, is eight and a half. Shlomki and his siblings are called Sabras because they were born in Israel.

Rivka, Shlomki's mom, is expecting a new baby. Everyone in his family is very excited.

For work, his mom teaches the Alexander Technique to students. This helps people to use their bodies more efficiently.

Rivka was born in Poland. When she was two, she came to Israel with her parents.

Brad, Shlomki's dad, was born in the United States. When he was eighteen, he left home and moved to Israel.

Shlomki's paternal great-great-grandfather was from Russia, and his grandparents on

his mother's side are from Poland. Jews traditionally have wandered around the world looking for a safe place to practice their religion within their community. Some Jewish families have lived in this area for more than two thousand years. Israel provides a homeland for Jews from all over the world.

Like Muhammad's dad, Brad also built his family's home.

He paints houses to make a living. He paints only the insides of buildings because the outsides of most houses in Israel are built from stone.

Shlomki has many pets. He has a goat called Iskey, two dogs named Puppy and Nojo, seven chickens, and seven ducks. From the goat's milk, his mother makes cheese and yogurt.

Dinner at Shlomki's house is a special time. To prepare for this meal, Rivka shops in the Jerusalem market because there are no stores in Nataf.

Smoked mackerel, avocado, apples, and cheese are some of Shlomki's favorite foods. Olives are eaten like potato chips. No one can eat just one!

Shlomki's family is not religious, but they do celebrate certain holidays. Hanukkah is Shlomki's favorite holiday because he gets to light the candles and eat Hanukkah doughnuts!

This is the Torah. It is the sacred text of the Jews. It is kept in the synagogue, and read from during Sabbath and holiday services. When a boy turns thirteen, he is expected to read from the Torah for his first time. This marks his passage into manhood.

Shlomki's best friend is Gidon Igra. They go to school together in Jerusalem.

Next year Shlomki's mom and dad have decided to send all their children to the same special school that Muhammad is going to. They believe that this school, with both Jewish and Arab students, will prepare their children for peace in the future.

Shlomki is scared to go to this new school. He will miss all his Jewish friends from his old school. He will especially miss Gidon. He has never had any Arab friends.

In September, school begins. Every day, Shlomki takes a van with other Jewish children from Nataf to his new school.

Muhammad also travels to school by van with Arab children from Abu Ghosh.

As they travel, they pass historical sites that remind them of the wars between Arabs and Jews. These ruined vehicles on the roadside were destroyed during the war in 1948.

Sometimes they pass soldiers, which always makes Muhammad and Shlomki fear new wars between Arabs and Jews.

High up on a hill sits a village called Neve Shalom/Wahat al-Salam. Both the Hebrew *Neve Shalom* and the Arabic *Wahat al-Salam* mean "oasis of peace." In this village, Arabs and Jews of Israeli citizenship choose to live and work together equally and in peace. There are twenty families who live here. The children of this community have their own school. It starts from nursery school and continues through sixth grade.

This year, for the first time, children from outside the community are going to this school.

Muhammad and Shlomki are among the first "outsiders" to go. Everyone in the village is very excited to meet them.

When Muhammad and Shlomki arrive, Arab and Jewish teachers greet them. These teachers created this school because of their belief in peaceful coexistence between Arabs and Jews.

Muhammad and Shlomki are in the same class. There are sixteen children in their class, half of them Arab, half of them Jewish.

In the beginning weeks of school, the Arab and Jewish children in their class admit and discuss their fear of each other. Because they speak different languages, the teachers translate their words.

The conflicts between Arabs and Jews have often led to violence between them. Muhammad and Shlomki listen and talk about their fears.

In this school, Muhammad and Shlomki learn about each other. They learn about their different religious celebrations and study their unique Arab and Jewish histories. This is one of the only schools that teaches Jews about Arabs, and Arabs about Jews. This year they are studying Jerusalem, the capital city of Israel. They will learn about its architecture, art, and history.

On a class trip, Shlomki is taken, for his first time, inside the Dome of the Rock, a religious site for all Moslems. Muhammad visits the Western Wall, all that remains of the first Jewish temple ever built.

Children's art of the Dome of the Rock and the Western Wall.

As they study about Jerusalem, they learn to write the word *Jerusalem* in both languages. Jerusalem is called *Al-Quds* (the Holy) in Arabic, and *Yerushalayim* in Hebrew.

During the beginning months of school, Muhammad and Shlomki want to talk to each other, but they cannot because Shlomki speaks only Hebrew and Muhammad speaks only Arabic.

In school, an Arab teacher, Anwar, patiently teaches Shlomki to read and speak Arabic.

Ety, a Jewish teacher, teaches Muhammad to read and speak Hebrew.

Both boys watch with envy as the young children in kindergarten who were raised in the Neve Shalom/Wahat al-Salam community talk in Arabic and Hebrew with ease and make friends with one another.

Shlomki and Muhammad work hard to learn each other's language. They want to know each other better, but talking is difficult. That makes it very hard for them to be friends.

Playing soccer is a language both boys understand. When Muhammad scores a goal, Shlomki runs over to him and shakes his hand. Muhammad feels great!

In English class, their teacher, Bob, teaches them the song "Michael, Row Your Boat Ashore." Muhammad and Shlomki laugh a lot about their terrible singing.

One day, Muhammad brings a picture of his new pet horse, Micky, to school and shows it to his class. As soon as Muhammad sits down, Shlomki moves his seat close to Muhammad.

"Can I come to your house and ride your horse?" Shlomki asks Muhammad in Arabic. Shlomki can hardly believe how easily the words have come to him.

"Yes," says Muhammad in Hebrew. "I would love that!"

Ety and Anwar, their teachers, watch them with delight! Muhammad and Shlomki have now learned their most important lesson. They are becoming friends.

On Saturday, Shlomki and his dad visit the Arab village of Abu Ghosh for their first time. They are greeted warmly by Muhammad's family.

At first Shlomki feels a bit strange. Muhammad's family is much larger than his. His house is much bigger. It is also hard to speak without teachers there to help them.

Muhammad's and Shlomki's dads begin talking in Hebrew about building houses. Muhammad's dad knows Hebrew. Shlomki's dad is teaching himself Arabic.

While the men talk, Shlomki and Muhammad decide to visit Micky, the horse.

Micky is not very friendly. He is not yet used to his new home at Muhammad's house, and he will not let them near him.

Both boys plead with Micky, in Hebrew and Arabic, to let Shlomki ride him, but Micky stays far away.

"I think Micky is afraid," says Shlomki in Arabic.

"Yes, I think you are right," Muhammad answers in Hebrew.

The boys speak softly to the horse. When they offer him an apple, Micky cautiously lets them pet him. They both realize that it will take some time before the horse trusts them enough to let them ride.

After lunch, Shlomki and Muhammad play by the pond with the ducks.

When the day ends, Muhammad and Shlomki have become great friends. They plan to get together next week so that Shlomki can visit with Micky again. They have struggled to speak in Hebrew and Arabic together. Sometimes they even speak English and invent their own sign language. But mostly they just laugh!

As the school year in Neve Shalom/Wahat al-Salam continues, many other new friendships are made. Muhammad and Shlomki's classroom bubbles with activities and play.

In this "oasis of peace," it is understood that friendship and understanding are the grounds on which peace can grow. Slowly, at Neve Shalom/Wahat al-Salam, peace and friendship bloom.

41

Faces of Israel

Israel is a diverse country with many different types of people. Jews have emigrated from all over Europe, Asia, North Africa, and North and South America to live there. Recently, many Jews came from Ethiopia.

Palestinian Arabs are Arabic-speaking people from the former land of Palestine. The last remains of Palestine were divided between Egypt, Jordan, and Israel as a result of the war in 1948. Among the Palestinian Arabs, there are Muslims, Christians, Druze, and others.

The Land

There are many different types of land in Israel: Deserts, canyons, fertile land, rocky hills, sandy beaches, and a salt lake below sea level. All can be found in this tiny country.

About Neve Shalom/Wahat al-Salam

In this strife-torn corner of the world known as the Middle East there is as much to give hope as there is to spread despair. Unfortunately, the hope doesn't get as much publicity.

Nestled on one of the peaks in the range of hills leading up to Jerusalem, this small community known as Oasis of Peace, or in Hebrew and Arabic as *Neve Shalom/ Wahat al-Salam* (NS/WAS), has been proving that when hope and trust are the common denominators among people, there is no time for despair — and dreams can come true.

NS/WAS is a cooperative village of Jews and Arabs of Israeli citizenship. The members of NS/WAS are demonstrating the possibility of coexistence by creating a social, cultural, and political community based on mutual acceptance, respect, and cooperation. This community is not a melting pot. Each individual remains faithful to his or her own cultural, national, and religious identity.

The children of this community have their own nursery, kindergarten, and primary school.

This primary school is the first comprehensive Arab/ Jewish school in Israel that is both bilingual and bicultural.

Just recently, NS/WAS has opened its kindergarten and primary school to thirty Arab and Jewish children from outside of the village. Muhammad and Shlomki are two of these children. Children come from the large Arab village of Abu Ghosh, and from Jewish communities in the area (Nataf/Castel and Kfar Uriah).

There are now a total of sixty children attending the NS/WAS school and kindergarten. Ultimately the village plans to extend its facilities to accommodate 150.

Another very important part of NS/WAS is its School for Peace, which conducts workshops for Arab and Jewish youth, students, educators, and others from all over Israel.

Here, Arabs and Jews find a rare opportunity to meet each other in an atmosphere conducive to intensive dialogue. The results are a deepened understanding of neighbors previously regarded with fear and hostility.

These workshops have served more than thirteen thousand Arab and Jewish high school students from Israel.

As a village, NS/WAS does not have a political charter, nor is it affiliated with any political party. The work of the village is educational.

For four consecutive years, Neve Shalom/Wahat al-Salam has been nominated for the Nobel Peace Prize.

History

Over the past 4,000 years, hundreds of wars have occurred in the land where Israelis and Palestinians live. It is there that the stories we read in the Bible took place. Judaism, Christianity, and Islam all have religious and historical ties to this region. While the people of the three faiths share Abraham's message of a single God, Abraham's land was to suffer a long history of conflict and war.

Whether the reasons be political, religious, national, or all three, tensions in this region continue. The story of Shlomki and Muhammad takes place in the background of the Jewish–Arab conflict; a conflict that exists both within Israel, and between Israel and her neighbors.

History — dates, names, places — appears to be objective, but the story of a country's events can be told in many ways because it is seen differently by the people who experienced it.

For example, the war between Arabs and Jews that happened in 1948 is referred to in different ways. For Jews, it is called the War of Independence because it resulted in the establishment of the State of Israel. For Palestinians, it marks the beginning of their diaspora, which means that many of their people fled or were driven out to live in other countries. Those who remained became Israeli citizens.

Since the war in 1948, Israel and her Arab neighbors have been caught in a continuing cycle of violence, which included an additional four wars. War in 1967 resulted in Israel's occupation of the Sinai peninsula, the West Bank, Gaza, and the Golan Heights.

In 1979 Egypt became the first Arab country to sign a peace treaty with Israel. Israel returned the Sinai to Egypt as a part of their agreement.

The West Bank and Gaza, however, are inhabited by over a million Palestinians who have been living under military occupation since 1967. Today much of the conflict is centered on the fate of these territories, and on the question of who is to control them. All of the sides involved share fear and mistrust of each other, which also affect the quality of relations between Jewish and Arab citizens of Israel. There are many different ways that people deal with these problems. Some may try to ignore them, others react with violence, and some seek a way to create dialogue with the other side.

In October, 1991, in Madrid, Spain, an event occurred that brings hope for peace to both Jews and Palestinians. Representatives of Israel, the Palestinians, and other Arab countries sat with one another for the first time to discuss peace. That was the first step in a long, difficult process of building peace that may give Jews and Arabs like Shlomki and Muhammad hope for a brighter future.

Glossary

ALLAH The Arabic name for God.

ARABIC A Semitic language spoken in the Arab countries.

DESCENDANT A child, a grandchild, a great-grandchild (etc.), of one specific person.

FASTING To eat nothing for a period of time.

HANUKKAH The Festival of Lights. Candles are lit for eight days to commemorate the victory of the Maccabees.

HEBREW The Semitic language of the ancient and modern Jews, which was used in the Old Testament, and is still spoken by Jews in Israel today.

ISLAM A religion based upon the belief in one god for whom Muhammad is messenger.

JEW A person who practices the Jewish religion.

JUDAISM The religion started by Abraham based on the belief in one god.

KORAN The sacred text of Islam containing the revelations made by Allah to Muhammad.

LABAN A thin, liquid yogurt.

MOSLEM A person who believes in or follows the religion of Islam.

MOSQUE A Moslem house of worship.

MUHAMMAD The messenger of Islam. The prophet Muhammad was born in Mecca, in the Arabian peninsula, in the year 570 A.D.

OASIS A fertile spot or area in a desert watered by a spring, stream, or well.

PEACE The absence of war or strife.

RAMADAN The ninth month of the Moslem year, spent fasting and praying from sunrise to sunset. It is a time for reflection and for showing kindness to others.

SABRAS Native-born Israelis named for the cactus fruit that is prickly on the outside and sweet on the inside.

SIBLING A brother or a sister.

TEMPLE The Jewish house of worship. Synagogue is another word for temple.

TERRITORY An area of land.

TORAH A parchment scroll containing the five books of Moses (the first five books of the Old Testament).

WAR Fighting between groups of people.

Hebrew/Arabic Language Comparison

Although Hebrew and Arabic are two different languages, many of their words look and sound alike. That is because their roots are the same. Both are Semitic languages. The Semitic people (who are chiefly Arabs and Jews) are descendants of Shem, Noah's eldest son.

English	Hebrew	Arabic
olive	זַיִת ZAH-yit	زيتون zey-TOON
boy	יֶלֶד YEH-led	ولد WA-lad
daughter	בַּת BAHT	بنت BINT
house	בַּיִת BAH-yit	بيت BEYT
eye	עַיִן ah-YEEN	عين EYN
head	רֹאשׁ RO'SH	رأس RAAS
hand	יָד YAHD	يد YAD
dog	כֶּלֶב KEH-lehv	كلب KALB
wind	רוּחַ ROO-ahch	رياح RE-yah
day	יוֹם YOM	يوم YOHM
night	לַיְלָה LY-lah	ليلة LEY-la
soap	סַבּוֹן sah-BONE	صابون Sa-BOON
peace	שָׁלוֹם shah-LOM	سلام sah-LAHM

Hebrew and Arabic are read from right to left!

Acknowledgments

We would like to pay tribute to those who helped with the telling of this story:

Sharon Burde from American Friends of Neve Shalom/Wahat al-Salam, for her generous support and belief in this project, which led to its fruition, and for helping to write the history at the back of the book.

The community of Neve Shalom/Wahat al-Salam, without whom there would be no story.

The Jabar and Frankin families, for their generous time, support, and patience.

Dianne Hess, my editor, for her encouragement and wisdom.

Marijka Kostiw, for her impeccable taste in designing this book.

Amatzia Dayan, whose tour throughout Israel left us properly awed and inspired.

Daphna Karta Schwartz and Shai Schwartz, who generously took us into their home and into their hearts.

Bob Mark, whose careful review of the text and sensitive input on matters of history and politics of the region were an invaluable resource.

Muhammad Mouaffaq Ghazal, for his worthy consultation.

Rama Vernon and Max Lafser of the United States Center for International Dialogue, whose counsel initiated this project.

North American Conference on Ethiopian Jewry, for two photographs on page 42.

William W. Hess for fact checking the manuscript.

Finally, I wish to thank Michal Zak, the Boulous family, Anwar Daoud, the Edlund family, Coral Aron, Aishe and Abed Najjar, Yazmine Abdid, Robert Altman, Temple Adas Israel, Ruth Marten, and Paul Bacon, for their special help and attention to this project.

Library of Congress Cataloging-in-Publication Data

Dolphin, Laurie.
Neve Shalom / Wahat al-Salam: Oasis of peace / by Laurie Dolphin;
photographed by Ben Dolphin.
p. cm.
Summary: Text and photos present the lives of two boys, one Jewish
and one Arab, who attend school in a unique community near Jerusalem where
Jews and Arabs live together in peace.
ISBN 0-590-45799-3
1. Jewish–Arab relations — Juvenile literature. 2. Jewish
children — Jerusalem — Juvenile literature. 3. Children, Palestinian
Arab — Jerusalem — Juvenile literature. 4. Neve Shalom (School) —
Juvenile literature. [1. Jewish–Arab relations.] I. Dolphin,
Ben, ill. II. Title. III. Title: Wahat al-Salam.
IV. Title: Oasis of peace.
DS119.7.D645 1993
303.48'2—dc20
92-15552
CIP
AC

12 11 10 9 8 7 6 5 4 3 2 1   3 4 5 6 7 8 9

Printed in the U.S.A.   44

First Scholastic printing, March 1993

Designed by Marijka Kostiw